MW00975576

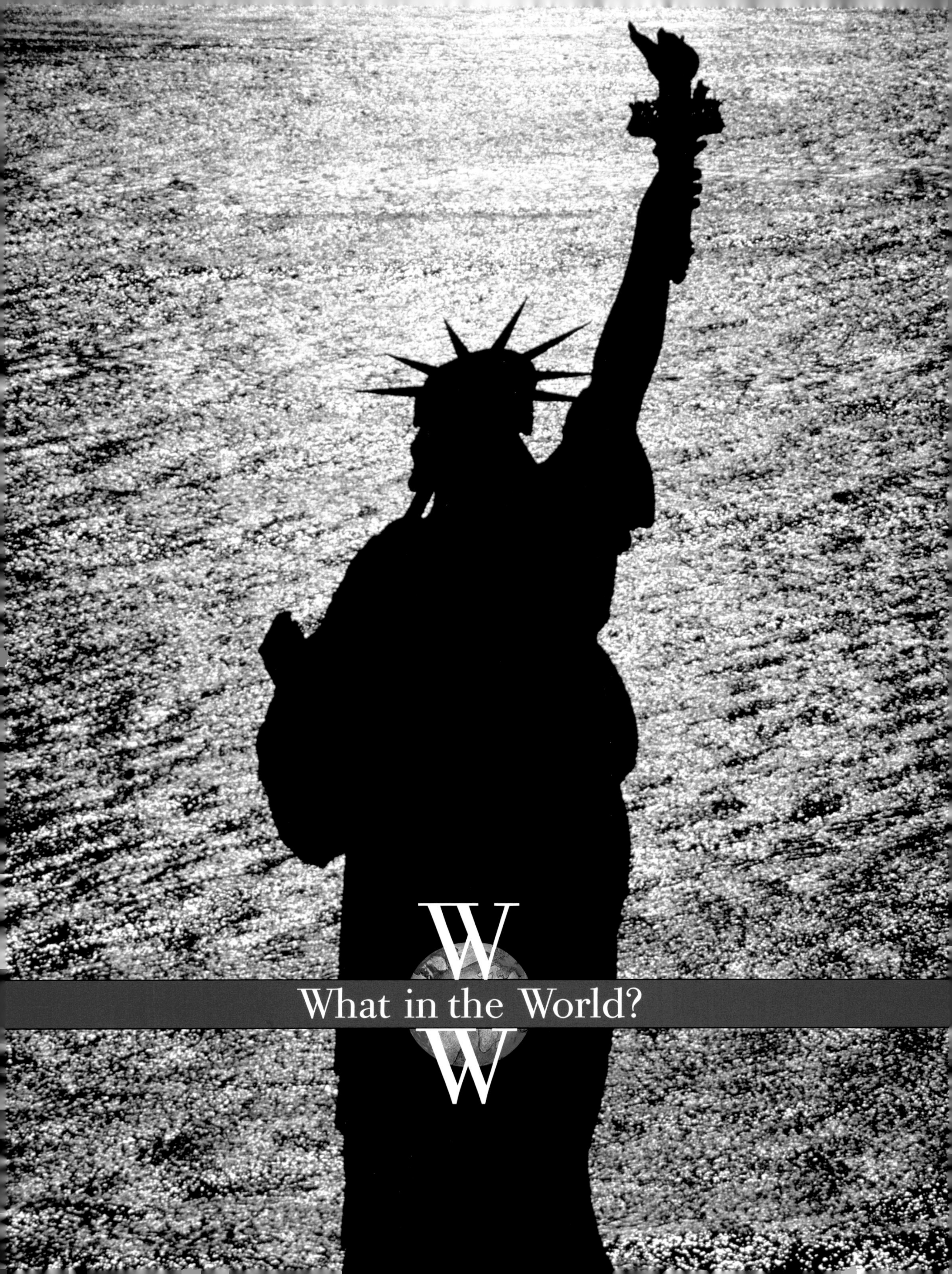
W
What in the World?
W

The Statue of Liberty

Jennifer Fandel

What in the World?

Creative Education

Introduction

In the morning sunlight of New York Harbor, as the ship he was riding drew near the American shore, a vision overcame Auguste Bartholdi. The year was 1871, and the Frenchman was traveling to the United States to propose a sculpture, a gift from France to celebrate the friendship between the two nations. Against the backdrop of the boat-filled harbor, Auguste imagined a colossal bronze figure reaching skyward and surrounded by waves. It would take 15 years for the vision to become reality—to become the Statue of Liberty, a monument that has carried her torch through both weather and time, and a symbol of freedom recognized around the world.

Many people have referred to Liberty as the eighth wonder of the world since the Colossus of Rhodes—a metal statue known to be smaller than Liberty—is considered among the world's seven ancient wonders.

The Statue of Liberty has been an icon of freedom for more than 120 years.

Silent and strong, the Statue of Liberty towers over all as she stands watch in New York Harbor.

The American Civil War put an end to slavery, liberating African-Americans.

Across the Distance

In the 1870s and 1880s, when Auguste Bartholdi was at work on the Statue of Liberty, the future was bright with promises of opportunity and freedom in many corners of the world. The United States, just out of the Civil War (1861–1865), vividly embodied these promises. President Abraham Lincoln's "Emancipation Proclamation" in 1862 had declared all African-American slaves free, and many now traveled north to find work in industrial cities. Many Americans headed west to find better land and mineral riches, and millions of European immigrants placed their feet on the soil of this growing nation. Among America's champions of freedom during this time was the tireless suffragist Susan B. Anthony, who led a determined campaign to give women the right to vote.

Suffragist Susan B. Anthony

Like America's cowboys, South America's gauchos *saw their niche decline in the late 1800s.*

In Central and South America, rugged cowboys roamed the lands, tied to little but their herds of cattle. These *gauchos* in South America (particularly Argentina) and *vaqueros* in Central America were the last of a dying breed. As Europe and North America became more industrialized, they turned to Central and South America to fulfill their food needs. As this business grew more profitable, cattle were rounded up on trains rather than on cattle trails, and the *gauchos* and *vaqueros* began fading into obsolescence.

In the late 1800s, Americans consumed large quantities of foreign goods such as bananas from Central America and coffee from Brazil. They also imported sugarcane and cigars from Cuba.

Coffee beans (left) and sugarcane (opposite) were valuable export crops.

Across the Atlantic Ocean, on the west coast of Africa, former American slaves settled in the independent republic of Liberia. In the first decades after their country's founding in 1847, Liberians struggled for stability as they built their nation and tried to establish new connections to their African past. At the same time, more and more kingdoms and tribes throughout Africa were falling to the influence of European colonization. In eastern Africa, the ancient kingdom of Ethiopia won a victory for freedom by resisting the colonization efforts of Italy and remaining independent.

To the east of Africa, in India, British rule helped strengthen India's educational and legal system. Before the British began educating the Indian people, only those who held high positions were educated. British reforms gave all people, including women, the right to learn. Along with basic skills such as reading and arithmetic, Indian children learned of European democracy. These lessons about equality, liberty, and justice would give Indians the strength to fight for freedom from the British at the turn of the 20th century.

Realism marked much of the literature of the late 1800s. Russian novelist Leo Tolstoy portrayed war's brutality in *War and Peace,* and *A Doll's House* by Norwegian playwright Henrik Ibsen contemplated equality between men and women.

An illustration (opposite) for Rikki Tikki Tavi, *Rudyard Kipling's classic tale of an English colonial family in India; playwright Henrik Ibsen (right).*

An 1888 poster from the U.S. presidential campaign of sitting president Grover Cleveland and his vice president, Allen Thurman.

In the late 1800s, people in eastern India lived in thatched-roof dwellings with wicker and mud-plastered walls. They bought their goods at bazaars where families showcased their skills at cloth weaving, basketry, pottery, or wood carving.

Hindu potters at work in India during the late 1800s.

The vaporetto, a motor-driven water bus, made its debut in Venice, Italy, in 1881. Many tourists still preferred to ride on the old-fashioned, romanticized gondola, a boat that relies on manpower for propulsion.

Venice's gondola was at its pinnacle in numbers and style in the late 1800s.

The new development of barbed-wire fencing boosted Australia's booming sheep ranching industry in the 1870s.

Across the Indian Ocean, discoveries of coal and minerals made Australia prosperous. The planting of drought-resistant wheat and sugarcane also boosted the country's economy. The most profitable industry, though, was sheep. Moving into the dry outback region, farmers set up large sheep ranches. In the late 1870s, Australia passed laws to establish an eight-hour workday and gave workers the right to unionize. This harmony between work and worker in Australia gave the growing country a reputation as a "workingman's paradise."

By the 1870s, the development of barbed wire made the sheep rancher's job in Australia much easier. With sheep no longer able to go astray, ranchers established bigger, more profitable businesses.

Rapid industrial growth in Sydney, Australia, was embodied by smoke-belching coal plants in the late 19th century.

The Impressionists first came together after Paris's Salon repeatedly rejected their work. Among these groundbreaking artists were France's Claude Monet, Auguste Renoir, and Camille Pissarro; England's Alfred Sisley; and America's Mary Cassatt.

Claude Monet's The Zuiderkerk at Amsterdam: Looking up the Groenburgwal.

Central and South America became active in exporting goods to industrial nations in the late 1800s. Brazil exported rubber from the Amazon rain forest, and Chile mined nitrates for fertilizers and explosives.

In Europe, meanwhile, the art scene was exploding. In Paris, France, art movements vied for attention, each one—Realism, Impressionism, and Post-Impressionism—reacting against the others. As the camera gained popularity, the Impressionists wanted to move away from what they felt was a stark, exact portrayal of the world. Instead, they tried to capture the fleeting movement of light and the spirit of a moment. Artists such as Auguste Renoir, Camille Pissarro, and Claude Monet flourished during these years.

Auguste Renoir, who began his artistic career as a porcelain painter at age 14, created The Girl at the Bank *(opposite) in 1875.*

When Parisian fashions such as the bustle took the world by storm in the late 1800s, women's posture often suffered.

Paris was Europe's fashion center in the 1870s. Wealthy women wore large bustles (padding at the back of large skirts) made of fox tails, kitchen dusters, wire cages, and down cushions.

In 1880, the Cologne Cathedral in Germany was completed after 634 years of construction. With twin spires that reached 515 feet (157 m) high, it became the largest Gothic cathedral in northern Europe.

But there was one artist in Paris who was not interested in capturing moments or fleeting notions. He thought in big ideas and saw with steadiness through the changes unfolding throughout the world. Auguste Bartholdi had visions that were solid and unmovable, shaped in metal and set in stone.

Auguste Bartholdi dreamt big, and none of his visions would be bigger than the Statue of Liberty.

A Colossal Vision

Frederic-Auguste Bartholdi was born in 1834 in Colmar, the capital city in the Alsace region of France. His father, a successful landowner and member of the city council, died when Auguste was two. His mother then moved with Auguste and his older brother, Charles, to Paris to be closer to relatives.

One of Bartholdi's most popular sculptures in France is *The Lion of Belfort*, a lion carved into the side of a cliff in the town of Belfort. It symbolizes the French resistance efforts against the Germans in the Franco-Prussian War.

The ownership of large pastures, farmlands, vineyards, and forests around Colmar ensured the Bartholdi family a comfortable life. Every summer, the family returned to Colmar's winding, narrow roads and flowered courtyards, settling into their four-story, white stone home filled with oil paintings and fine furniture. But it was more than just the easy lifestyle and Colmar's slow pace that appealed to Auguste. It was the spirit of the Alsatian people—their patriotism, independence, and pride—that made him regard Colmar as his home. This passion for his homeland would inspire much of Auguste's work.

Bartholdi's famous homeland sculpture, The Lion of Belfort.

This sculpture outside of the Musée Bartholdi in Colmar, France, honors the visionary behind the Statue of Liberty.

Growing up in Paris, Auguste was surrounded by beautiful architecture and public sculpture. His mother encouraged his interest in art at an early age, and he studied painting, drawing, architecture, and sculpture with many renowned Parisian artists in his late teens. Although he eventually gravitated toward sculpture, Auguste would use skills from all of the arts to design, plan, and create his projects. At school in Paris, Auguste also met the American painter John LaFarge, who would remain a lifelong friend. This friendship helped Auguste make connections in America and would later lead to Auguste's marriage to a cousin of the LaFarge family, a French woman named Jeanne-Emilie Puysieux.

In 1853, at the age of 19, Auguste had his first sculpture exhibited at the famous Salon, a yearly exhibition of art in Paris. At 21, he received his first commission: a bronze sculpture of General Jean Rapp, a native of Colmar. He pursued further commissions with zeal, convincing government officials and important statesmen that his combination of talent and patriotism produced sculpture of beauty and merit.

In 1869, Bartholdi proposed a design to the nation of Egypt for a colossal lighthouse at the entrance of the Suez Canal. The plan for the lighthouse, which was to be shaped like a woman carrying a torch, was rejected because of its cost.

Of his art, Bartholdi said that he wished "to engrave [his] name at the feet of great men and in the service of grand ideas." Bartholdi's perspectives on art separated him from many fellow artists who created art to express themselves.

Painter John LaFarge became Bartholdi's friend and an important American contact.

Selection to exhibit at Paris's yearly Salon art show was considered validation of an artist's work.

Bartholdi, an up-and-coming sculptor, displayed his first sculpture at the government-sponsored Salon exhibition in 1853.

In 1856, 22-year-old Auguste traveled to Egypt, where he laid eyes on the first colossal sculptures he had ever seen. The monuments of Abu Simbel, enormous figures of ancient gods carved into sandstone cliffs, filled Auguste with wild ambition. There on the banks of the Nile River, staring into stone faces carved more than 3,000 years before, Auguste decided that he, too, wanted to create a monument that expressed infinite ideas through sheer size.

The colossal statues of pharaoh Ramesses II at Abu Simbel (opposite); the Great Sphinx of Giza (below).

The French-American friendship behind Liberty dated back to the American Revolutionary War, when French soldiers fought alongside the Americans. In turn, the American government gave financial assistance to France in the French Revolution and Franco-Prussian War.

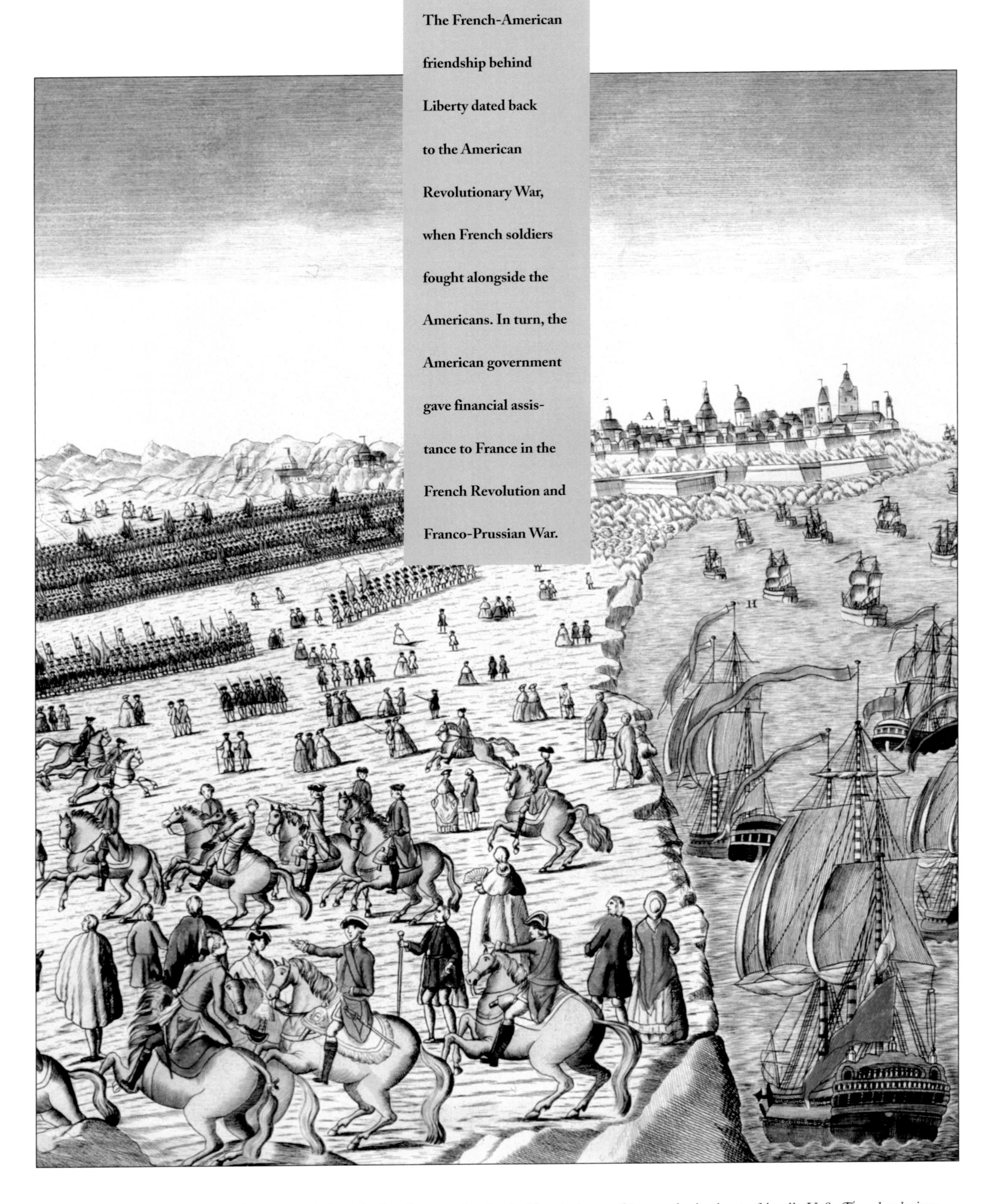

In 1781, a fleet of French ships bolstered American patriots in the Revolutionary War—a beginning to friendly U.S.-French relations.

Over the next 10 years, Auguste continued to dream big while working steadily on commissioned sculptures of celebrated French military figures. In 1865, while attending a dinner party hosted by Edouard de Laboulaye, a French professor and statesman who studied American history, Auguste overheard discussion of a statue to commemorate French-American friendship and the United States' inspirational idea of liberty. The discussion, which afterwards continued to linger in the back of Auguste's mind, took on special significance while the sculptor served as a French officer in the Franco-Prussian War (1870–1871).

The 1870 painting The Bombardment of Paris *offers a glimpse of the Franco-Prussian War in which Bartholdi served.*

The outcome of the war filled Auguste with grief. His homeland of Alsace was taken over by the Germans, and many Alsatians fled their homes, refusing to live under German rule. His mother refused to leave their home, even though the Germans had invaded it and seemed inclined to stay. To know that the Alsatian people had lost their freedom gave Auguste a sense of purpose, and he went to de Laboulaye and asked for both his permission and support to undertake the French-American statue project. In 1871, with letters of introduction in hand, 37-year-old Auguste boarded a ship for his first trip to America.

Bartholdi's homeland (above), as depicted by Frenchman Charles Kuwasseg in the painting A River View in Alsace; *towns on the French-German border (opposite) suffered frequent ruin during the many wars of the last two centuries.*

In the U.S., Auguste traveled the country and met with President Ulysses S. Grant, influential senators, editors of prominent New York newspapers, and common citizens to assess American support for the project. The short, dapper Frenchman with the immaculate suits, honest face, and twirled mustache made a positive impression on the Americans. Auguste's passion for the project was rivaled only by his excitement for this young country. As he traveled by stagecoach and train, Auguste was stunned by the variety of landscapes—mountains, deserts, prairies, and rolling hills—and impressed by the bold people who faced many hardships to make these lands home.

It is believed that Bartholdi sculpted Liberty's face with his mother's face in mind. After their homeland of Alsace was taken over by the Germans after the Franco-Prussian War, Bartholdi saw his mother's stern face as a symbol of repressed freedom.

Bartholdi was impressed with America's wide open spaces and the bold ambitions of its free population.

To Auguste, the immensity of the land and its determined people made America the perfect home for his great dream of a colossal sculpture. The Statue of Liberty would become the largest structure of the time—surpassing the heights of America's newly introduced skyscrapers—and the largest metal sculpture ever created.

From the beginning, Bartholdi envisioned his sculpture to be a highly visible and inspirational beacon of freedom.

Workers exacted painstakingly careful measurements as the Statue of Liberty was constructed piece by piece.

French chemist Louis Pasteur

In 1881, in a workshop in the heart of Paris, the steady beat of hammers echoed, and white plaster dust filled the air. Amid the ruckus, a team of craftsmen was methodically transforming Auguste's four-foot (1.2 m) study model of Liberty into a colossal figure that would ultimately rise 151 feet (46 m) high.

French chemist Louis Pasteur tried an experimental rabies vaccine on a nine-year-old boy from Alsace, France, in 1885. The boy, Joseph Maister, lived through the treatment, proving the new vaccine successful.

To avoid structural problems in the sculpture, Auguste enlarged his study model in increments, making corrections and adjustments along the way, until it was 36 feet (11 m) high. Next, the statue was divided into smaller sections, and each part was enlarged four more times its size. From these final enlargements, carpenters constructed intricate wooden molds covered with plaster. To ensure accuracy, the carpenters took an average of 9,000 measurements for each section.

Copper was Auguste's metal of choice for the statue's outer shell because it was not as expensive or heavy as bronze. Once the molds were completed, the copper shell of the statue was shaped. Using a rare, ancient technique called repousse, craftsmen hand-hammered large sheets of copper the thickness of a penny over every mold. Out of flat copper, the various pieces of Liberty—her curving lip, a finger, and the ripples of her gown—emerged.

Repousse is a metal-working process invented by the Greeks. In their statue work, the ancient Greeks found that they could hammer metal thinner than they could cast it in a mold.

By the winter of 1882, Bartholdi's Parisian warehouse was filled with many different pieces of Lady Liberty in progress.

The Statue of Liberty's index fingers are eight feet (2.4 m) long, and her mouth spans three feet (1 m) across. The seven points of her crown represent the seven continents and seven seas.

Gustave Eiffel, known in his native France as "Le Magicien du Fer" ("The Magician of Iron"), used his genius with metal to build the Eiffel Tower—a structure commemorating the 100th anniversary of the French Revolution—in 1889.

As Auguste watched Liberty's outer shell take shape, Gustave Eiffel—a Frenchman known for his visionary works of engineering—worked on the statue's internal framework. Aware that Liberty would have to withstand high coastal winds, Eiffel designed a unique support system. Large iron beams reinforced by crossbeams stood at the center of her "skeleton." Iron braces branched out from this central support, and individual pieces of Liberty's copper shell would be riveted to each brace. This distributed the copper's weight to points throughout the central support structure. Most importantly, it allowed the copper shell to expand and contract due to temperature changes—or bend in the wind—without putting strain on the entire statue at once.

With her seven-spiked crown and serious expression, Liberty embodies an unconquerable spirit.

Once the inner structure and copper shell were completed in the spring of 1883, 49-year-old Auguste and his crew moved to an adjacent courtyard to assemble the statue. Craftsmen climbed immense scaffolding as they riveted 25 tons (23 t) of iron together to form Liberty's skeleton. They then riveted her copper pieces to the iron braces. A few months later, the completed Liberty towered over the tallest apartment buildings of the Paris neighborhood, sunlight glinting off her copper.

On Auguste's first visit to the United States in 1871, he had proposed a deal to American lawmakers. The French people would raise the money for the statue, and Americans would raise the funds for the pedestal on which it would stand. By 1882, the French people had donated the approximately $250,000 necessary to complete the statue. Although the U.S. still hadn't raised the $300,000 necessary to build the pedestal by the spring of 1885, Auguste believed America would honor its commitment. The sculptor and his craftsmen dismantled the finished Liberty and packed her into 214 crates for the journey across the Atlantic.

Craftsmen who worked on Liberty felt compelled to leave their signatures on her, and many engraved the rivets with their names. Bartholdi, likewise, engraved a "B" for Bartholdi on the first copper plate to be riveted.

Throughout his life, Bartholdi was haunted by the declining health of his older brother, Charles. His brother, who was also an artist, became mentally ill in his 30s and once tried to throw Auguste from a train. Charles died a year before Liberty was unveiled.

U.S. postage stamps bearing Lady Liberty have been common since the statue rose in New York Harbor.

Liberty made a brief appearance in the heart of Paris, raising her torch above pedestrian buildings.

Joseph Pulitzer, Union soldier in the Civil War, journalist, and father of the Pulitzer Prize, raised money for Lady Liberty's pedestal.

Around this time, an American newspaper owner named Joseph Pulitzer began a pedestal fund-raising campaign. Believing that New York's rich should donate the remaining funds, Pulitzer launched frequent attacks on the wealthy in his newspaper, *The World*, hoping to shame them into action. When that failed, he turned to the masses for support. Pulitzer promised to print donors' names, messages, and dollar amounts in his paper. The plan worked. In only five months, 120,000 donors raised the remaining $100,000, much of it in sums of $1 or less.

Joseph Pulitzer, a Hungarian immigrant who arrived in America in 1864, made his living in the newspaper business. In 1917, he established the Pulitzer Prize, an annual prize honoring American achievements in journalism, literature, and the arts.

When asked to write a sonnet for the pedestal fund-raising efforts, American poet Emma Lazarus at first declined. But after seeing the poor condition of immigrants as they reached America's shores, she composed the poem "The New Colossus" in 1883.

Sonnets.

I.

The New Colossus.

Not like the brazen giant of Greek fame,
With conquering limbs astride from land to land;
Here at our sea-washed, sunset gates shall stand
A mighty woman with a torch, whose flame
Is the imprisoned lightning, and her name
Mother of Exiles. From her beacon-hand
Glows world-wide welcome; her mild eyes command
The air-bridged harbor that twin cities frame.
"Keep, ancient lands, your storied pomp!" cries she
With silent lips. "Give me your tired, your poor,
Your huddled masses yearning to breathe free,
The wretched refuse of your teeming shore.
Send these, the homeless, tempest-tost to me,
I lift my lamp beside the golden door!"

1883.
(Written in aid of Bartholdi Pedestal Fund.)

Emma Lazarus's original poetry manuscript for "The New Colossus."

Bedloe's Island was renamed Liberty Island in 1956. The 10-acre (4 ha) island, located two miles (3 km) off the Manhattan coast, was once the home of Fort Wood, a military post used for harbor fortifications.

Except for the wives of dignitaries, women weren't allowed at the 1886 unveiling of the Statue of Liberty. In protest, suffragists cruised on boats near the island, giving speeches about the injustice of women being denied voting rights.

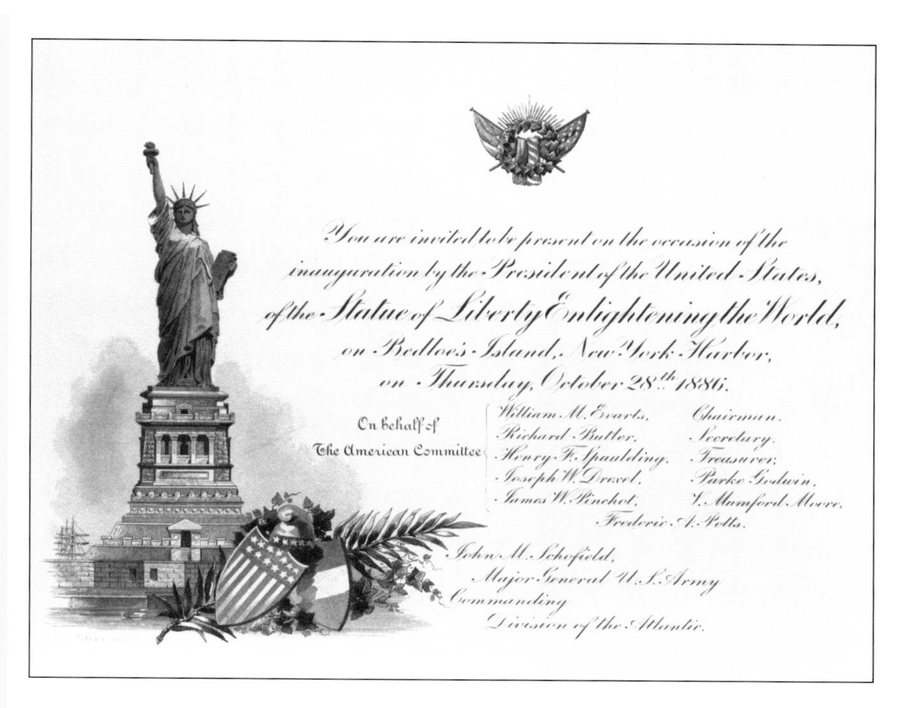
You are invited to be present on the occasion of the inauguration by the President of the United States, of the Statue of Liberty Enlightening the World, on Bedloe's Island, New York Harbor, on Thursday, October 28th 1886.

On behalf of The American Committee

William M. Evarts, Chairman.
Richard Butler, Secretary.
Henry F. Spaulding, Treasurer.
Joseph W. Drexel,
Parke Godwin,
James W. Pinchot,
J. Mumford Moore,
Frederic A. Potts.

John M. Schofield,
Major General U.S. Army
Commanding
Division of the Atlantic.

An official invitation to the unveiling of the Statue of Liberty.

In 1883, the Orient Express began operation. Connecting Paris, France, to Constantinople, Turkey, the railroad brought the cultures of the Middle East and Asia closer to Europe.

After arriving in New York Harbor in the summer of 1885, Liberty sat until the pedestal was finished the following spring. Designed by Richard Morris Hunt, a well-known American architect, the 89-foot-tall (27 m), white granite pedestal took eight months to construct as workers poured cement and laid the granite blocks. The reassembly of Liberty took only four months, and on October 28, 1886, in front of thousands of spectators, she was unveiled on Bedloe's Island. The gas lamps that illuminated her torch were lit that night.

Edward Moran commemorated Liberty's groundbreaking ceremony with his 1886 painting Unveiling of the Statue of Liberty *(opposite).*

The earliest name for the Statue of Liberty was "Liberty Enlightening the World," given to her by French statesman Edouard de Laboulaye. Through the years, she has also been called "Lady with the Lamp" and "Lady Liberty."

Although she looks almost diminutive against New York's modern skyscrapers, Lady Liberty stands as proudly today as ever.

In 1916, Gutzon Borglum, the sculptor of Mt. Rushmore, re-sculpted Liberty's flame to let more light out. During remodeling for her 1986 centennial, a new flame shaped like Bartholdi's original was made out of gold leaf.

Liberty's torch is a symbol for enlightenment, and it was originally planned that people be able to view New York from her highest point.

Against the backdrop of Manhattan's modern skyscrapers, the Statue of Liberty still stands proudly, her bright copper now weathered to a blue-green patina. Among the billowing folds of Liberty's gown, there is motion. She strides forward, breaking the shackles around her feet. In her left hand, she clutches a thick tablet inscribed with the date of American independence, July 4, 1776. And in her right, she holds her torch high, lighting the way toward freedom. In 1903, at a time when European immigrants were streaming into the U.S. in record numbers, a plaque of Emma Lazarus's poem "The New Colossus" was affixed to Liberty's pedestal. In its most famous lines, Liberty speaks to those first entering America:

Give me your tired, your poor,

Your huddled masses yearning to breathe free,

The wretched refuse of your teeming shore.

Send these, the homeless, tempest-tost to me,

I lift my lamp beside the golden door!

Through the poem, another vision of Liberty was born. Immigrants with sea-weary eyes gazed upon a strong mother figure that not only championed liberty, but also welcomed them to a new land of opportunity. Through war, weather, and time, her lamp has blazed the way ever since.

At the Statue of Liberty's unveiling, U.S. President Grover Cleveland promised to honor the symbolism of the statue, saying, "We will not forget that Liberty has here made her home, nor shall her chosen altar be neglected."

The *S.S. Columbia* was the first steamship to feature incandescent lights. In May 1880, during its maiden voyage to San Francisco, the ship was lit with 115 Edison lamps.

When Grover Cleveland dedicated France's gift, crowds cheered to welcome and thank those responsible for the new American icon.

A. BARTHOLDI
LIBERTY
US
RF

W

What in the World?

W

1834 Frederic-Auguste Bartholdi is born in Colmar, France.

1840 The world's first adhesive postage stamps, featuring Queen Victoria's portrait, are sold in England.

1845 Ireland's potato crop fails, and famine sweeps the country, triggering Irish immigration to America.

1853 Bartholdi exhibits his work for the first time in Paris's Salon.

1861–1865 The U.S. Civil War is fought; it results in the deaths of 620,000 soldiers.

1869 The book *20,000 Leagues Under the Sea,* by French author Jules Verne, is published.

1870 The Franco-Prussian War breaks out; it will last through the following year.

1874 The first exhibition of Impressionist paintings opens in Paris.

1876 Bartholdi marries Jeanne-Emilie Puysieux while on his second visit to the United States.

1877 Tokyo University is founded in Japan and becomes the country's most prestigious educational institution.

1879 American inventor Thomas Edison perfects the incandescent light bulb.

1881 Bartholdi begins the enlargement process on the Statue of Liberty.

1884 The world's first roller coaster opens at Coney Island, New York.

1884 Gustave Eiffel completes engineering for the Statue of Liberty's interior structure.

1885 The French ship *Isere*, carrying the Statue of Liberty, arrives in New York Harbor.

1886 The Statue of Liberty is unveiled.

1888 Kodak introduces the camera to America, making photography widely available to the masses.

1890 The first electric underground trains in London, England, begin service.

1903 The poem "The New Colossus" is affixed to the Statue of Liberty's pedestal.

1904 Bartholdi dies of tuberculosis in Paris.

Copyright

Published by Creative Education
123 South Broad Street, Mankato, Minnesota 56001

Creative Education is an imprint of The Creative Company.
Design by Rita Marshall
Production design by The Design Lab

Photographs by Art Resource, NY (Timothy McCarthy), Corbis (Alan Schein Photography, Andy Warhol Foundation, Bettmann, John Carnemolla/Australian Picture Library, Steve Chenn, Christie's Images, Fine Art Photographic Library, Christel Gerstenberg, Historical Picture Archive, E.O. Hoppé, Dave G. Houser, Bob Krist, Museum of the City of New York, Gianni Dagli Orti, Philadelphia Museum of Art, PITCHAL FREDERIC/CORBIS SYGMA, PoodlesRock, Chris Rainier, Reuters, Leonard de Selva, Underwood & Underwood, Ron Watts)

Library of Congress Cataloging-in-Publication Data
Fandel, Jennifer.
The Statue of Liberty / by Jennifer Fandel.
p. cm. — (What in the world?)
ISBN 1-58341-377-4
1. Statue of Liberty (New York, N.Y.)—History—Juvenile literature.
2. Bartholdi, Frâdâric Auguste, 1834-1904—Juvenile literature. 3. New York (N.Y.)—Buildings, structures, etc.—Juvenile literature. I. Title.
II. Series.

F128.64.L6F36 2005 974.7'1—dc22 2004058228

First Edition
9 8 7 6 5 4 3 2 1

Index

Africa 11
American Civil War 7
Anthony, Susan B. 7
Australia 14
Bartholdi, Auguste
  at work 7, 33, 34, 35, 36
  birth 20
  homeland 20
  travels to Egypt 25
  travels to the U.S. 30, 36
Bedloe's Island 41
Brazil 8, 17
Cassatt, Mary 17
Central America 8, 17
Colmar, France 20
Eiffel, Gustave 35
European colonization 11
Franco-Prussian War 26, 27, 28
Hunt, Richard Morris 41
Ibsen, Henrik 11
Impressionists 17
India 11, 13
Laboulaye, Edouard de 27, 28
LaFarge, John 22
Lazarus, Emma 39, 44
Lincoln, Abraham 7
Monet, Claude 17
Paris, France 17, 19, 22
Pulitzer, Joseph 39
Realism 17
Renoir, Auguste 17
Salon 17, 22
South America 8, 17
Statue of Liberty
  creation of 33–35, 39, 41
  funding for 36
  unveiling of 41, 44
Venice, Italy 13